Learn Spanish Like a Native *for Beginners* - Level 1

Learning Spanish in Your Car Has Never Been Easier! Have Fun with Crazy Vocabulary, Daily Used Phrases, Exercises & Correct Pronunciations

www.LearnLikeNatives.com

© **Copyright 2020 By Learn Like A Native**

ALL RIGHTS RESERVED

No part of this book may be reproduced, stored in a retrieval system, or transmitted in any form or by any means, without the prior written permission of the publisher.

CONTENTS

INTRODUCTION 1

CHAPTER 1 – THE FIRST IMPRESSION IS VERY IMPORTANT 11

CHAPTER 2 – ARE WE RELATED? 21

CHAPTER 3 – WHAT DAY IS IT? 30

CHAPTER 4 – THERE IS NO GIFT LIKE THE PRESENT. 44

CHAPTER 5 – HAVE A LOOK AROUND 58

CHAPTER 6 – HOW FAR CAN YOU COUNT? 69

CHAPTER 7 – WHAT DID YOU WANT TO BE WHEN YOU GROW? 77

CHAPTER 8 – WHERE ARE WE GOING? 89

CHAPTER 9 – SURVIVAL 101 97

CHAPTER 10 – WHAT IS THE COLOR OF THE SKY? 103

CHAPTER 11 – SO MUCH TO DO, SO MUCH TO SEE 110

CHAPTER 12 – I HAVE A LITTLE CRAVING 120

CONCLUSION 131

Introduction

Benefits of Learning Spanish

It is easy to stick with your native tongue. As an English speaker, you may feel as if you have a considerable advantage. But have you not ever been fascinated by other languages? By different cultures? Do you not find them captivating?

Let's say you are going to your holiday destination (maybe Spain, or even just a Spanish-speaking country). Did you think of everything? First aid kit, papers, and documents? Very good, but what about your foreign language skills? Have you ever thought about how you will express yourself? Unfortunately, many travelers neglect this topic and believe that with English, you can get anywhere. Some also assume you can communicate well with your hands and feet. The question you should ask yourself, though, is:

What do I expect from my journey, and which goals do I have (besides just relaxing, of course)?

To give you a little motivation, here are five advantages to being able to express yourself in the language of the country you are in:

- You get to know the locals much more authentically
- You understand the culture and attitude of people much better
- You can negotiate more effectively
- You do not waste valuable time, because you can communicate faster
- You feel safer

Just to keep it short, you do not have to learn a foreign language to perfection.

A Bit of History About This Beautiful Language...

We know Spanish as a poetic language. There's something about the way the string of words sounds like. It is as if it is meant to woo a lover.

This is why you may be surprised to discover that Spanish was actually derived from Vulgar Latin, the kind of Latin spoken by Roman soldiers. By 200 BC, this form of Latin became more popular and widespread throughout the Empire. Vulgar Latin gave birth to Spanish and other romantic languages we know today - Italian, French, Romanian, and Portuguese.

The Perfect Method

I'm sure you've been told there's no right or wrong way to learn a language. Well, that can't be right, because it's wrong! The truth is, most people don't lack in motivation, drive, excitement, determination, or even talent. More than anything, people lack the correct method.

I've been learning and teaching languages my whole life, and I've realized that the number one reason why people get stuck learning any language is simple. It's not because they are lazy, it's not because they don't have time, it's because they are bored!

You could go to the best schools and have the best teachers in the world, but if you're bored in your Spanish class, you're unlikely to get anywhere. Starting from scratch and ingesting new knowledge and can be a daunting thing as it is. So, if you're not fully engaged, learning a new language will be a long road.

Think about it. You've been a child before. Did you learn grammar before you knew how to speak? Of course not! So why do that now? In my opinion, that's where most language methods fail. Because they get caught up in all the specific rules and formal details a language holds, before worrying about whether or not their students understand what's going on. What's the point in knowing irregular verbs, if you can't even order food at the restaurant! My point being, unless you're planning to write a Ph.D. in Spanish, the most important thing for you is to be able to speak with other people.

That's where Learn Like A Native comes in!

With approximately 90 million people who speak and study Spanish as a non-native language, there's plenty of opinions as to what the best way to learn is.

That's why I based my method on modern expert research. The latest studies show that the most efficient way to learn languages – and Spanish in particular – is by learning vocabulary and grammar in conversation.

Using this method, I'll teach you how to apply formal knowledge in a real-life environment, through practical and relatable materials. With short and fun lessons, you'll stay engaged every step of the way, helping you retain vocabulary much more efficiently.

www.LearnLikeNatives.com

The audiobook version is narrated by a Spanish native speaker who will get you comfortable with the sounds of the language. You'll take an active part in the learning process and be required to speak, repeat, and exercise new sounds as they come up throughout the lessons.

Don't simply listen passively, but instead learn actively by practicing tough sounds such as the double "r," like a true native Spanish-speaker. If you have any trouble, the textbook will help you with written sounds so you can visualize letters and the sound they relate to.

You'll feel like you're in a Spanish class. But one you can take everywhere! With only 10 to 20 minutes per lesson, you can focus on each topic independently without any stress. Squeeze them into your schedule, sitting in your car or waiting for the Bus, and enjoy the flexibility of going through each step at your own pace. No one is watching you, of course, but I trust you'll do the work!

Learning a new language is a complex and rich experience. After you are done with this book, you will be ready (or more prepared) to travel, immerse yourself in Spanish-speaking cultures, read fiction and newspapers in Spanish, watch films, eat Latin American and Spanish foods, learn recipes, make Spanish-speaking friends, and, most importantly, enjoy

www.LearnLikeNatives.com

yourself! This book is inspiring and vibrant to read and/or listen to, motivating you to speak and embrace the Spanish language, no matter how new, intermediate, or advanced you are to it.

Before you know it, you'll find yourself having a full-blown conversation in Spanish and wonder how you got there!

Are you ready? Okay, then we can start. Whichever language level you achieve depends entirely on you.

www.LearnLikeNatives.com

www.LearnLikeNatives.com

FREE BOOK!

Get the *FREE BOOK* that reveals the secrets path to learn any language fast, and without leaving your country.

Discover:

- The **language 5 golden rules** to master languages at will

- Proven **mind training techniques** to revolutionize your learning

- A complete step-by-step guide to **conquering any language**

www.LearnLikeNatives.com

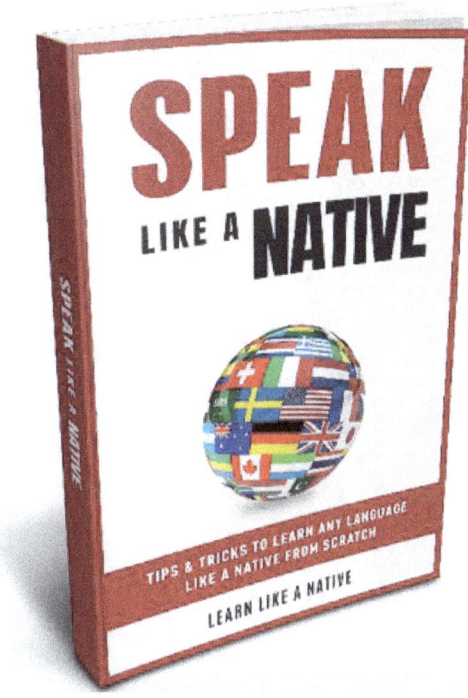

www.LearnLikeNatives.com

www.LearnLikeNatives.com

Chapter 1 – The First Impression Is Very Important

Everyone knows the old saying, "You only get one chance to make a good first impression."

Therefore, it's no surprise that one of the first things every child learns is to say hello and introduce themselves. Even J.K. Rowling, the famous author of that young wizard's adventures, said "A good first impression can work wonders", and I completely agree.

Just a simple "Hello" can make all the difference in a conversation. That's exactly the reason why we will begin this exciting adventure with Spanish greetings. You will learn how to introduce yourself, greet people at different times of the day, and many other useful things.

We will start with the most popular greetings. There are several ways to greet people in Spanish, depending on who you are addressing and whether you want to be formal or not.

www.LearnLikeNatives.com

Ready to start? I really hope you are as excited as I am!

So, let's begin with the most common ways to greet someone in Spanish:

| Hello. | Hola. |

Oh-lah

| Good morning. | Buenos días |

Boo-eh-nos-dee-us

Just like in English, saying "Good morning" in Spanish is a compound expression, which also has different variables depending on the time of the day you are.

That way, you can find these other expressions.

| Good afternoon. | Buenas tardes. |

Boo-eh-nus-tar-des.

This is a good starting point for us. Tahr-des is a short but tricky word because that will help you perfect your pronunciation. You will have to "adjust" some of your consonants, starting with "t" and "r".

Spanish "t" sounds a lot like a British "t". It has a stronger sound, which concentrates on the tip of your tongue. Try it out loud: "t".

Now, the Spanish "r" is a bit more difficult. Especially because Hispanics have two sounds for it: one for a simple "r" and one for a double "r". Let us work for a second on the basics, and we will build it from there.

To make a Spanish "r", follow these instructions.

1. Lift your tongue inside your mouth, until the tip is somewhere between your incisive upper teeth and your hard palate.

2. Take a breath in and then breathe out –strongly- through your mouth. This should make your tongue move a bit, like a flapping. If it does not move, relocate your tongue until you find the spot.

3. Repeat again, until you master it.

4. Practice this until you are making a sound that is similar to a cat purring.

5. Once you have achieved this, start graduating the amount of air you use. This is important because the difference between a simple and double "r" depends on the amount of air you put into it.

How did it go for you? Do not worry if it doesn't work straight away. I couldn't do these sounds for a long time, but practice makes perfect and eventually, you too will be able to obtain beautiful and clear "r's".

Going back to our lesson, we have "Good night".

| Good night. | Buenas noches. |

Boo-eh-nus-noh-chess

As for a goodbye, "Buenas noches" is also valid, and recommended in the case of formal and more respectful gatherings. It is similar to the word "aloha". As you may know, Hawaiians only use one word for both "hello" and "goodbye", which is "aloha". In a similar way, in Spanish, most greetings can also be used for both hello and goodbye.

You should also remember that, depending on whether you are greeting a friend or a stranger, you would use a different salutation.

For example, when entering a restaurant in the evening (or in any other formal occasion), you will say "Buenas noches" if you want to sound polite. Although, you can use "Hola" if you are meeting some old friends or greeting someone you already know (informal occasion).

| How are you? | ¿Cómo estás? |

Koh-moh-s-tahs-too

You may have noticed that there is no literal translation, and the word "you" is not translated. While in English the pronoun is always used, in Spanish the ending of the verb usually makes it clear who the subject is, so no pronoun is necessary.

Asking "Cómo estás?" is a really good way to start a friendly conversation. It is an informal greeting and can also be used between people you are familiar with to ask about their health or mood.

| How can I help you? | ¿Cómo puedo ayudarte? |

Koh-moh-poo-eh-doh-a-iu-dar-the

At this point, you have probably figured out the connection between two words: "how" and "cómo", and you know how important this word is in any language. This word is also important: "cuál".

| What is your name? | ¿Cuál es tu nombre? |

Koo-al-s-too-num-breh

An alternative to this phrase is "¿Cómo te llamas?", which is used just as often.

Koh-moh-te-ya-mus

To say what your name is in Spanish you use:

| My name is | Mi nombre es |
| **My name is** John. | **Mi nombre es** John. |

Me-num-breh-s

I am	Yo soy
I am new around here.	**Yo soy** nuevo por aquí.

Io-Soy

Thanks/Thank you.	Gracias.

Gra-cee-us

"Gracias" is used to say both "thanks" or "thank you". However, if you wish to show more gratitude, you could say "thanks to you", which translates to "Gracias a ti".

Gra-cee-us-ah-tee

I am sorry.	Lo siento.

Loh-see-n-toh

Nice to see you again.	Me alegra verte de nuevo.

Meh-ah-leh-gra-bur-teh-the-noo-eh-boh

www.LearnLikeNatives.com

Was it too hard? Don't worry. Greetings are basic phrases you will need to memorize, but I promise that the next sentences will be shorter and easier to remember.

| What is new? | ¿Qué hay de nuevo? |

Ke-eye-the-noo-eh-boh

Another sentence with a similar meaning is "¿Qué me cuentas?" which directly translates to "What do you say?"

Ke-meh-ku-n-tus

| How are you doing? | ¿Cómo te va? |

Koh-moh-the-vah

| Goodbye. | Adiós. |
| **Goodbye**. I love you. | **Adiós**. Te amo. |

Ah-dee-os

This is a short way to say "bye". However, as already mentioned, if you want to be more formal, you can use "Good morning/afternoon/night", or "Hasta luego".

See you later.	Hasta luego
Great! See you later.	**¡Genial! Hasta luego.**

Us-tah-loo-eh-goh

How are you sounding? Are you making sure to make a clear "t"? I hope so!

See you in a few.	Te veo más tarde.
Ok! See you in a few.	**¡Ok! Te veo más tarde.**

Ok-teh-be-oh-mus-tar-deh

As you might know, "Ok" is an English expression. Nevertheless, it's universally used worldwide, even among Spanish speakers. You should be aware, however, that there is a Spanish equivalent as well:

Ok.	Está bien.

Us-tah-bee-n

How is it going? Are you finding it difficult or is it easy? Maybe you need to practice a little bit more. Remember: practice is the key to mastery! Anyway, before we move to another topic, let's take a look at a short conversation that uses some of the words we have just learned.

Vendor   *Good morning!*

   Buenos días.

John: *Good morning to you, too.*

   Buenos días para usted también.

Vendor: *How can I help you?*

   ¿Cómo puedo ayudarle?

John: *I am here to pick up a cake.*

   Estoy aquí para buscar un pastel.

Vendor: *Sure. What is your name?*

   Claro. ¿Cuál es tu nombre?

John: *My name is John Hill.*

   Mi nombre es John Hill.

Vendor: *Oh, I am sorry. Your birthday cake is not ready yet.*

   Oh, lo siento. Tu pastel de cumpleaños no está listo aún.

John: *Ok. When can I come pick it up?*

Está bien. ¿Cuándo puedo venir a recogerlo?

Vendor: *It will be ready in one hour.*

Estará listo en una hora.

John: *Great. I will run some errands and come back.*

Genial. Haré unas diligencias y regresaré.

Vendor: *Thanks for understanding. See you in a few.*

Gracias por entender. Te veo más tarde.

John: *Sure. See you later!*

Claro. ¡Hasta luego!

I hope John doesn't get low blood sugar, because he will have to wait for a while. In the meantime, shall we go and learn some new words and phrases that relate to family and relatives? This could be really handy if you were going to John's birthday party!

www.LearnLikeNatives.com

Chapter 2 – Are we related?

I am sure your family loves telling the story of your first word.

Language acquisition starts with receptive language, the understanding of sounds and words of the world around us. There is a good chance that either "mum" or "dad" (or a variable of these) was the first word you learned

Dad	Papá
My **dad** went out to get more ice.	Mi **papá** salió a conseguir más hielo.

Pah-páh

Accent marks are very important in the Spanish language. They can seem insignificant, but those tiny marks can completely change the meaning of a word. The accent on the à in "papà" - short on the first syllable and hard accent on the second, just as it happens with "mamá".

Mom	Mamá
My **mom** is there, by the corner.	Mi **mamá** está ahí, en la esquina.

Mah-máh

Son	Hijo
My **son** used to play tennis.	Mi **hijo** jugaba tenis.

E-ho

Daughter	Hija
My **daughter** likes to dance.	A mi **hija** le gusta bailar.

E-ha

In Spanish, there are two genders: every noun must be either masculine or feminine. hijo/hija is a good example. As a preliminary guide, it is good to know that singular:

- Nouns ending in "o" are masculine (male), with few exceptions;

- Nouns ending in "a" are nearly all feminine (female).

Throughout this book, we will see several examples of these. As a general rule, you can form the feminine or masculine version of nouns by changing the final vowel.

Therefore, you would use words like "hija" or "ellas" for females, and "hijo" or "ellos" for males.

Brother	Hermano
This is my **brother** Alex.	Este es mi **hermano** Alex.

Ehr-ma-no

Sister	Hermana
She is my **sister** Coreen.	Ella es mi **hermana** Coreen.

Ehr-ma-na

www.LearnLikeNatives.com

Uncle	Tío
I have two **uncles**.	Yo tengo dos **tíos**.

Tee-os

In the same way, as in English, in Spanish you form most plurals by simply adding an "s" to the end of every word. Just like you change from "uncle" to "uncles", you get a plural by turning "tío" into "tíos".

Aunt	Tía
My **aunt** has two kids.	Mi **tía** tiene dos hijos.

Tee-a

Cousin	Primo
My **cousin** lives far away from here.	Mi **primo** vive lejos de aquí.

Pree-mo

Grandfather	Abuelo

| My **grandpa** picked up mangoes every day. | Mi **abuelo** recogía mangos todos los días. |

Ah-boo-eh-loh

Grandmother	Abuela
My **grandma** loved knitting.	Mi **abuela** amaba tejer.

Ah-boo-eh-lah

How is it going so far? Don't you worry, we just need to meet a few more people, and then we can take a short break.

Siblings	Hermanos/Hermanas
I have three **siblings**.	Yo tengo tres **hermanos/hermanas**.

Ehr-ma-nos/ Ehr-ma-nas

Relatives	Parientes

| I have many **relatives**. | Yo tengo muchos **parientes**. |

Pah-ree-en-tes

This is a great word to practice your single "r". Remember that you create this the same way you do it for the double "r", but the amount of air that you breathe out is considerably lower, and it produces a softer sound.

Family	Familia
My **family** is big.	Mi **familia** es grande.

Fah-ee-lee-ah

Neighbor	Vecino
Dan is a great **neighbor**.	Dan es un gran **vecino.**

Beh-see-noh

How do you feel? Ready for a short practice? Great!

Allyson: *Happy birthday!*

¡Feliz cumpleaños!

Kelly: *Hello! Thanks a lot! I am happy that you came.*

¡Hola! ¡Muchas gracias! Estoy feliz de que hayas venido.

Allyson: *I am happy that you invited me.*

Yo estoy feliz de que me hayas invitado.

Kelly: *Sure. Let me show you who everyone is.*

Claro. Déjame mostrarte quién es todo el mundo.

Allyson: *Great!*

¡Genial!

Kelly: *That girl is my sister, and my cousin John is sitting next to her.*

Esa chica es mi hermana, y mi primo John está sentado junto a ella.

Allyson: *Yeah. Next to them is your brother Mark, right?*

Sí. Junto a ellos está tu hermano Mark, correcto?

Kelly: *Perfect! Yes. He picks me up from school sometimes.*

¡Perfecto! Sí. Él me recoge de la escuela algunas veces.

Allyson: *I remember.*

Lo recuerdo.

Kelly: *Good. By that other corner are grandma, grandpa and uncle Ed.*

Bien. En esa otra esquina están la abuela, el abuelo y el tío Ed.

Allyson: *Your grandma looks so young!*

¡Tu abuela luce tan joven!

Kelly: *Yes. I hope I have the same luck.*

Sí. Yo espero tener la misma suerte.

Allyson: *Don't we all?*

¿No lo deseamos todas?

Kelly: *Let's see... who's missing? Oh, well. Dad is outside, with the neighbors and the rest of the family.*

Veamos... ¿quién falta? Oh, bueno. Papá está afuera, con los vecinos y el resto de la familia.

Allyson: *Great! I can't wait to meet them.*

¡Genial! Yo no puedo esperar a conocerlos.

So, what do you think? Learning a new language is about listening to things over and over again and repeating many times. My advice is to always say the words out loud. This is an excellent way to practice a new language and, if you do so, you will see a significant improvement over the next chapters.

Chapter 3 – What day is it?

Learning how to measure and tell the time is hugely valuable. In many cultures, punctuality is extremely important and viewed as a form of respect, and I personally think it is a great sign of courtesy. Of course, learning the days of the week and months is also important, so you can make plans. Another thing you may want to know before leaving for a foreign country is what season is it, to know what to pack and dress accordingly.

As always, we will start with the basics:

Second	Segundo
One hour has sixty **seconds**.	Una hora tiene sesenta **segundos**.

Seh-goon-dos

Minute	Minuto
One hour has sixty **minutes**.	Una hora tiene sesenta **minutos**.

Mee-noo-tos

Hour	Hora
There are twenty-four **hours** in a day.	Hay veinticuatro **horas** en un día.

Oh-ras

An excellent moment to practice that single "r". Repeat with me: oh-ras. Good, let's continue.

Day	Día
January has thirty-one **days**.	Enero tiene treinta y un **días**.

Dee-us

Week	Semana
We have one **week** to finish.	Tenemos una **semana** para terminar.

Seh-mah-nah

Month	Mes

| We will be there next **month**. | Nosotros estaremos allá el **mes** próximo. |

Mess

Year	Año
It's the wedding of the **year**!	Es la boda del **año**!

Ah-nioh

Spanish has the "ñ" sound. Compared to an "n", this sound is very nasal.

To master the "ñ", you should start by pronouncing a "nioh" sound but really into the tip of your tongue. A perfect "ñ" sound resonates between your hard palate, the tip of your tongue and your nose. This is how you can start doing it.

1. Pronounce an "n" and maintain that sound. Feel how it resonates in the back of your mouth.

2. Now, try to take that sound "forward" by pushing it behind your upper teeth. Create a "nioh" sound if you need it. You will feel how it starts moving into the tip of your tongue.

3. Repeat as many times as you need.

Decade	Década
This **decade** is going to start soon.	Esta **década** va a empezar pronto.

The-ka-tha

Century	Siglo
This is the discovery of the **century**.	Este es el descubrimiento del **siglo**.

See-gloh

Morning	Mañana
The meeting was this **morning**.	La reunión fue esta **mañana**.

Mah-niah-nah

Afternoon	Tarde
Will you be there in the **afternoon**?	¿Tú estarás ahí en la **tarde**?

Tar-the

How is that double "r" sound going? Great! Let's keep moving.

Night	Noche
The moon comes out at **night**.	La luna sale en la **noche**.

Noh-che

Spring	Primavera
Everything flowers in **spring**.	Todo florece en **primavera**.

Pree-ma-veh-rah

Remember: that soft sound you need for "rah" will depend on the amount of air that you breathe out.

Summer	Verano
We had a fun **summer**.	Nosotros tuvimos un **verano** divertido.

Beh-rah-noh

Autumn	Otoño

| Look at the first **autumn** leaf. | Mira la primera hoja de **otoño**. |

Oh-to-nioh

Winter	Winter
Winter has arrived.	Ha llegado el **invierno**.

In-bee-er-noh

January	Enero
January is the first month of the year.	**Enero** es el primer mes del año.

Eh-ne-roh

February	Febrero
That tree flowers in **February**.	Ese árbol florece en **Febrero**.

Feh-breh-ro

| March | Marzo |

March is a good month for harvesting.	**Marzo** es un buen mes para cosechar.

Mar-soh

April	Abril
We stop activities in **April**.	Nosotros paramos las actividades en **Abril**.

Ah-breel

Have you noticed how most of the names of the months are similar between English and Spanish? That's a relief, right?

May	Mayo
May is going to be a great month.	**Mayo** será un gran mes.

Ma-ioh

June	Junio
The break starts in **June**.	El descanso comienza en **Junio**.

Hu-neo

July	Julio
July is a hot month in Spain.	**Julio** es un mes caliente en España.

Hu-lee-oh

August	Agosto
This **August** will be rainy.	Este **Agosto** será lluvioso.

Ah-gos-toh

September	Septiembre
Next semester starts in **September**.	El próximo semestre comienza en **Septiembre**.

Sep-tee-m-breh

October	Octubre
My birthday is in **October**.	Mi cumpleaños es en **Octubre**.

Ok-too-breh

November	Noviembre
We celebrated Halloween all **November**.	Nosotros celebramos Halloween todo **Noviembre**.

Noh-bee-m-breh

December	Diciembre
The year ends in **December**.	El año termina en **Diciembre**.

D-c-m-breh

Monday	Lunes
Today is **Monday**.	Hoy es **Lunes**.

Loo-ness

Tuesday	Martes
I have an appointment next **Tuesday**.	Tengo una cita el próximo **Martes**.

Mar-tess

Repeat again: mar-tess. This is a great word to practice the double "r" and the "t" sound. Remember that the Spanish "t" is very clear and strong, like the British one.

Wednesday	Miércoles
Wednesday is not a good day for me.	El **Miércoles** no es un buen día para mí.

Mee-er-ko-less

Thursday	Jueves
I'll see you next **Thursday**.	Yo te veré el próximo **Jueves**.

Hu-eh-ves

Friday	Viernes
The party is next **Friday**.	La fiesta es el próximo **Viernes**.

Bee-er-ness

Saturday	Sábado
I play every **Saturday**.	Yo juego cada **Sábado**.

Sah-bah-doh

Sunday	Domingo
We can have breakfast this **Sunday**.	Podemos desayunar este **Domingo**.

Do-meen-goh

How is it going? Are you ready for a short conversation?

Ally: *So, what are your plans for the next year?*

Así que, ¿cuáles son tus planes para el año que viene?

Juan: *I honestly don't know what will happen after winter.*

Yo honestamente no sé qué pasará luego del invierno.

Ally: *Will you at least come back in February? Spring is lovely here.*

¿Al menos vendrás en Febrero? La primavera es hermosa acá.

Juan: *If I don't, I promise I will be back to celebrate summer, in July.*

Si no lo hago, prometo que regresaré para celebrar verano, en Julio.

Ally: *Everyone loves summer. I love autumn.*

Todo el mundo ama el verano. Yo amo el otoño.

Juan: *Why?*

¿Por qué?

Ally: *Leaves change colors and I love the weather between September and November.*

Las hojas cambian de color y amo el clima entre Septiembre y Noviembre.

Juan: Two weeks ago you weren't loving it that much.

Hace dos semanas no lo estabas amando mucho.

Ally: Are you talking about that rainy Wednesday? I hated that.

¿Estás hablando de ese Miércoles lluvioso? Yo odié eso.

Juan: Yeah. As if it were not enough with those boring Mondays.

Sí. Como si no fuese suficiente con esos aburridos Lunes.

Ally: Oh, sure. I don't like Mondays. I love Fridays.

Oh, seguro. No me gustan los Lunes. Yo amo los Viernes.

Juan: Like everyone. But I like Saturdays better.

Como todo el mundo. Pero a mí me gustan más los Sábados.

Ally: Yes. Especially the ones in Spring, when you take your boat for a ride.

Sí. Especialmente los de Primavera, cuando sacas tu bote a dar un paseo.

Juan: You remember it. Good.

Tú lo recuerdas. Bien.

It's not as hard as you thought, right? There is a lot to remember, but sometimes it's easier if you find the similarities between English and Spanish, like as those in the names of the months. Again, practice makes perfect.

Now has come the time to learn some important verbs and how to conjugate them.

Chapter 4 – There is no gift like the Present

Just as in any other language, Spanish verbs are an important part of everyday speaking. When studying a foreign language, the present is the first tense you will learn, as this will allow you to form simple sentences. It is used to describe something that is happening right now or a state of being. Using the present tense, you will be able to speak about your desires, interests and plans.

First of all, in Spanish, verb conjugation is done by changing the ending of the verb. Verbs are divided into 3 different categories, called "conjugaciones" - conjugations. Each one is characterized by a specific ending in its infinitive form:

- First conjugation: Verbs ending in -AR (like amar)

- Second conjugation: Verbs ending in -ER (like creer)

- Third conjugation: Verbs ending in -IR (like vivir)

www.LearnLikeNatives.com

In this chapter I will teach you how to conjugate the regular verbs.

In addition, as you do in English, also in Spanish you can merge all the 3rd person singular pronouns. For your convenience, this is what we will do here.

Hopefully, with a bit of practice, you will realize that Spanish verb conjugation is actually much easier than it seems.

So, let's get started. There is no time like the present!

To love	Amar	Root	Termination
I love	Yo amo	Am-	Ar changes for "o"
You love	Tú amas		Ar changes for "as"
He/She/It loves	Él/Ella/Eso "ama"		Ar changes for "a"
We love	Nosotros amamos		Ar changes for "amos"

You love	Ustedes aman		Ar changes for "an"
They love	Ellos/Ellas aman		Ar changes for "an"

The root of all regular verbs never changes. As you can see, the root is the part preceding the infinitive ending. So, for example, in "Amar" the root is "Am-". Like we said, the root always remains the same, and different endings are added to denote the person, number or tense. Let's look at some examples.

I love the rain.	Yo amo la lluvia.
She loves the music.	Ella ama la música.
You love movies.	Ustedes aman las películas.
They love to play music.	Ellas aman tocar música.

Great! Here is a tip: using the above table you will be able to conjugate every other regular verb that ends in "-ar", all you have to do is add to the root the relevant ending, as we just did. Clearly, the same logic applies to verb of the second and third conjugation (-Er and -Ir). That's good to know, right?

Here are a few more examples. For the verb "to sing" - "cantar", you can separate the root "Cant-", and all you will need to do is to add the correct ending, as previously explained. The root of the verb "to eat" – "comer" is "com-", and for the verb "to share" - "compartir", the root is "compart-".

Think about what you like to do in your free time for a moment. What are your interests? What are you passionate about? Verbs are important to discuss all of these things.

To believe	**Creer**	**Root**	**Termination**
I believe	Yo creo	Cre-	Er changes for "eo"
You believe	Tú crees		Er changes for "es"
He/She/It believes	Él/Ella/Eso cree		Er changes for "e"

We believe	Nosotros creemos		Er changes for "emos"
You believe	Ustedes creen		Er changes for "en"
They believe	Ellos/Ellas creen		Er changes for "en"

You believe in loyalty.	Tú crees en la lealtad.
He believes in what he can touch.	Él cree en lo que puede tocar.
You all believe in yourselves.	Ustedes creen en ustedes mismos.
They believe in you.	Ellos creen en ustedes.

For verb "Creer" the root is "Cre-".

Following this rule, the actual change for the 1st person conjugation would be "Yo creeo". However, in Spanish we often employ contractions —as we tend to shorten many words. This way "Creeo" becomes "Creo". This is the only special case for this section.

So, what have you learned and what do you believe in? Repeat with me: "yo creo en....". Eventually, you will be able to better express yourself in Spanish, but –in the meantime- "yo creo en" is good enough.

Let's carry on with another important verb: "to live" – "Vivir". In this case, the root is "Viv-".

To nourish	Vivir	Root	Termination
I live	Yo vivo	Viv-	Ir changes for "o"
You live	Tú vives		Ir changes for "es"
He/She/It lives	Él/Ella/Eso vive		Ir changes for "e"
We live	Nosotros vivimos		Ir changes for "imos"

You live	Ustedes viven		Ir changes for "en"
They live	Ellos/Ellas viven		Ir changes for "en"

I live downtown.	Yo vivo en el centro.
She lives far away from here.	Ella vive lejos de aquí.
It lives on our rooftop.	Eso vive en nuestra azotea.
They live for singing and dancing.	Ellos viven cantando y bailando.

Now let's look at the present of the auxiliary verb "to be" – "ser". This verb is one of the most versatile, and you will use it a lot in Spanish: to introduce yourself, find out more about something or someone, describe places and things, etc. It is an auxiliary verb and its purpose is to help other verbs conjugate in compound tenses. In other words, it helps to create more complex sentences and tenses.

There is also another verb that can sometimes be used with the same meaning of "to be": "estar" – "to stay". While in English "to stay" is only used to describe your location, in Spanish it can also be used to describe a state of being.

That sounds complicated but let's break it down.

In Spanish, "verbo ser" applies in the following cases:

- When identifying or defining something. Like in "I am Latin-American" -"Yo soy Latino Americano"-, or in "I am Lucy" –"Yo soy Lucy".

- When describing something or someone's characteristics. As in "He is tall" – "Él es alto", or "They are smart" – "Ellos son listos".

- When locating the occurrence of an event, like "The meeting will be at my house" –"La reunión será en mi casa", or "The dinner is at five" –"La cena es a las cinco".

- When talking about the time of the day, weather, and such. As in "It is two at noon" –"Son las dos del mediodía", or in "It is summer" –"Es verano".

On the other side, we use "verbo estar" in these cases:

- When setting people and things in space. "I'm on the top of the world" –"Estoy en la cima del mundo"; "The shirt is on the bed" –"La camisa está sobre la cama".

- When talking of the state of something. "I am depressed" –"Estoy deprimido"; "She is pregnant" – "Ella está embarazada".

I know it may sound a bit confusing, but once you understand the differences, you will soon see how easy these are to use and how helpful they are to express yourself.

For the time being, let's see how to conjugate them.

To be	Ser	Estar
I am	Yo soy	Yo estoy
You are	Tú eres	Tú estás
He/She/It is	Él/Ella/Eso es	Él/Ella/Eso está
We are	Nosotros somos	Nosotros estamos
You are	Ustedes son	Ustedes están

| They are | Ellos/Ellas son | Ellos/Ellas están |

Here are some examples of the verb "essere".

I am a fanatic.	Yo soy un fanático.
She is a bit short.	Ella es un poco baja.
The party is around nine.	La fiesta es alrededor de las nueve.
It is two in the morning.	Son las dos de la mañana.

We have described someone and talked about the time.

Now, let's see some examples of the "verbo estar".

You are in the right place.	Tú estás en el lugar correcto.
She is worried.	Ella está preocupada.
We are alive.	Nosotros estamos vivos.

They are on table 5.	Ellos están en la mesa 5.

How does this sound? This will come with practice, so let's continue.

Alongside the verb "to be", the second most important verb in the Spanish language is "to have" – "Tener" –. It is an auxiliary and irregular verb that allows you to express numerous things: possessing something (literally or in a figurative way), communicate needs and desires, etc.

To have	**Tener**
I have	Yo tengo
You have	Tú tienes
He/She/It has	Él/Ella/Eso tiene
We have	Nosotros tenemos
You have	Ustedes tienen

| They have | Ellos/Ellas tienen |

I have a meeting.	Yo tengo una reunión.
It has big paws.	Eso tiene patas grandes.
We have a plan.	Nosotros tenemos un plan.
They have a place by the lake.	Ellos tienen un lugar junto al lago.

Are you looking forward to putting this into practice?

Emma: *Hi. I am Emma.*

Hola. Yo soy Emma.

David: *Nice to meet you. I am David.*

Encantado de conocerte. Yo soy David.

Emma: *Tell me, David. What do you like to do?*

Dime, David. ¿Qué te gusta hacer?

David: *I enjoy sailing on weekends.*

Yo disfruto navegar los fines de semana.

Emma: *Do you have a boat?*

¿Tú tienes un bote?

David: *Yes, I do. And what do you like to do?*

Sí, lo hago. ¿Y qué te gusta hacer?

Emma: *I have a dancing academy. I love to teach.*

Tengo una academia de baile. Yo amo enseñar.

David: *Really? I have a niece. She loves to dance.*

¿En serio? Yo tengo una sobrina. Ella ama bailar.

Emma: *Great! How old is she?*

¡Genial! ¿Cuántos años tiene?

David: *She is 6 years old. She turns 7 in two weeks.*

Ella tiene 6 años. Cumple 7 en dos semanas.

Emma: *I teach from the age of 7. Maybe you could bring her.*

Yo enseño a partir de los 7. Tal vez podrías traerla.

David: *Awesome. I am sure she will love it.*

Fabuloso. Estoy seguro de que le encantará.

As you can see, it is very important to know how to conjugate the Present simple. Just keep practicing until you achieve a better understanding.

Chapter 5 – Have a look around

Now, have a look around the room and tell me what you see. What's all around you? For instance, I usually keep a bottle of water on my desk and I always carry my mobile phone and wallet. In this chapter we will learn the names of a few things that you will probably have in your house.

Clock	Reloj
My **clock** says it is late.	Mi **reloj** dice que es tarde.

Reh-loh

Remember what we said at the beginning about punctuality? You will need a "reloj" to be always right on time.

Light	Luz
Turn the **light** on.	Enciende la **luz.**

Loose

Money	Dinero
Spend your **money** wisely.	Gasta tu **dinero** sabiamente.

Dee-neh-roh

Bed	Cama
This **bed** is comfortable.	Esta **cama** es cómoda.

Ka-mah

Window	Ventana
That **window** points south.	Esa **ventana** apunta al sur.

Venn-tah-nah

Water	Agua
I want some **water**.	Quiero un poco de **agua**.

A-goo-a

Car	Auto
That is a nice **car**.	Ese es un buen **auto**.

Au-to

Bicycle	Bicicleta
I took your **bicycle**.	Yo tomé tu **bicicleta**.

B-c-cleh-tah

Photo	Fotografía
I have your **photo** in my wallet.	Yo tengo tu **fotografía** en mi billetera.

Pho-to-gra-fee-a

News	Noticias
Did you read the **news**?	¿Tú leíste las **noticias**?

No-t-c-us

"Noticias" are very important to keep you informed. Let me give you a little advice. When preparing to visit another country, you should start reading local news sources from that place a couple of weeks before you get there. That will give you an insight into what is happening in the country and – why not – also some great talking points when you are speaking with locals.

Bin	Contenedor

I put it all in that **bin**.	Yo lo puse todo en ese **contenedor**.

Kon-teh-neh-door

Toothbrush	Cepillo de dientes
I need a new **toothbrush**.	Yo necesito un nuevo **cepillo de dientes**.

Seh-pee-io-deh-dee-n-ts

Mirror	Espejo
That **mirror** looks dirty.	Ese **espejo** se ve sucio.

S-peh-jo

Laptop	Ordenador portátil
You can use my **laptop**.	Tú puedes utilizar mi **ordenador portátil**.

Or-deh-nah-dor-por-tah-teel

Computer	Computadora

| That is my **computer**. | Esa es mi **computadora**. |

Kom-poo-tah-door-a

| Cellphone | Teléfono celular |
| I can't find my **cell phone**. | No encuentro mi **celular**. |

Ce-llu-lar

| Id | Identificación |
| Please, let me see your **ID**. | Por favor, déjame ver tu **identificación**. |

E-den-tee-fee-ka-sion

| Driving license | Licencia de conducir |
| You look funny in your **license**. | Tú te ves gracioso en tu **licencia de conducir**. |

Lee-cn-ce-a-the-kon-doo-cir

| Wallet | Billetera |

www.LearnLikeNatives.com

| Did you find your **wallet**? | ¿Encontraste tu **billetera**? |

Be-ye-teh-ra

Are you ready to create your own list? How many of those things are there in your house? Ok, let's use an example.

Nancy: *Honey! Do you have everything you need for camp?*

¡Cariño! ¿Tienes todo lo que necesitas para el campamento?

Peter: *Yes, mom. I think so.*

Sí, mama. Yo creo que sí.

Nancy: *Do you have your ID and phone?*

¿Tienes tu identificación y teléfono celular?

Peter: *Yes… I can't find my toothbrush.*

Sí. No puedo encontrar mi cepillo de dientes.

Nancy: I saw it near the bathroom mirror.

Lo vi cerca del espejo del baño.

Peter: Thanks! Can I bring my laptop?

¡Gracias! ¿Puedo llevar mi ordenador portátil?

Nancy: To camp? No! Bring your wallet. You need that.

¿Al campamento? ¡No! Lleva tu billetera. Necesitas eso.

Peter: I need money, too.

Necesito dinero, también.

Nancy: It is on your bed.

Está sobre tu cama.

Peter: Good. I also need water and a small container.

Bien. También necesito agua y un contenedor pequeño.

Nancy: A container? Why?

¿Un contenedor? ¿Por qué?

Peter: *For the food. Haven't you read the news? It's bear season.*

Para la comida. ¿Tú no has leído las noticias? Es temporada de osos.

Nancy: *Really? Ok. Keep your light close to you, just in case.*

¿De verdad? Ok. Mantén tu luz cerca de ti, por si acaso.

Peter: *Sure. Thanks, mom.*

Claro. Gracias, mamá.

I guarantee that if you follow the instructions and keep repeating our little lessons, you will make rapid progress and will soon be able to communicate fluently in Spanish. Feel free to go back to the previous chapters as many times as you like, all it takes sometimes is just a little something to jog your memory!

If you need help to count how many times you are repeating a sentence, move on to the next chapter: we are going to learn numbers next!

www.LearnLikeNatives.com

FREE BOOK!

Get the *FREE BOOK* that reveals the secrets path to learn any language fast, and without leaving your country.

Discover:

- The **language 5 golden rules** to master languages at will

- Proven **mind training techniques** to revolutionize your learning

- A complete step-by-step guide to **conquering any language**

www.LearnLikeNatives.com

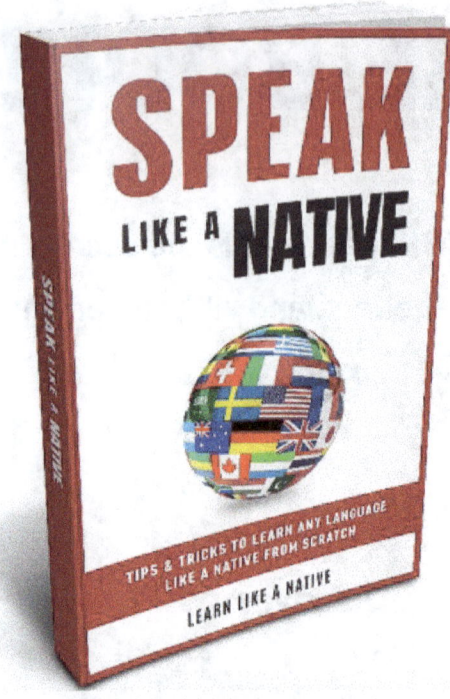

Chapter 6 – How far can you count?

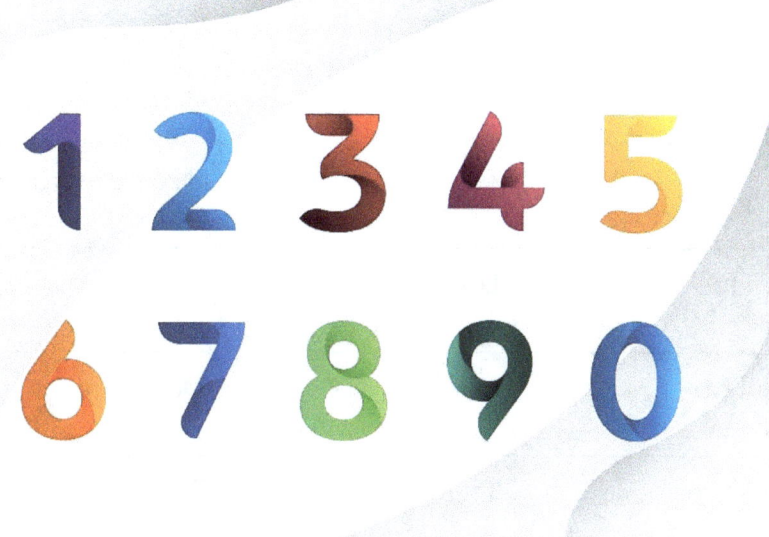

There are many nursery rhymes that help to introduce numbers even before a child understands numbers or how to count. It was probably through one of these songs that many of us learned numbers!

Don't worry. You won't have to do any math, just number learning!

When speaking in Spanish, you will often need to use and understand numbers to express time, record dates and – of course – count. So, here is a table to help you memorize them:

First, let's go with cardinal numbers. These numbers help us count objects.

		Pronunciation
One	Uno	Uh-noh
Two	Dos	Dos
Three	Tres	Tres
Four	Cuatro	Kua-troh
Five	Cinco	Sin-ko
Six	Seis	Seh-is
Seven	Siete	Si-eh-teh
Eight	Ocho	Oh-cho

Nine	Nueve	Noo-eh-beh
Ten	Diez	Dee-S
Eleven	Once	On-se
Twelve	Doce	Doh-se
Thirteen	Trece	Tre-se
Fourteen	Catorce	Ka-tor-se
Fifteen	Quince	Kin-se

As you can see, all the numbers from one to fifteen are specific words, and as such, you will have to learn it by heart. Let's see what happens from sixteen to nineteen.

Sixteen	Dieciséis	Dee-eh-si-seh-is
Seventeen	Diecisiete	Dee-eh-si-si-eh-te
Eighteen	Dieciocho	Dee-eh-si-oh-cho

| Nineteen | Diecinueve | Dee-eh-si-noo-eh-be |

Can you see that there is a pattern? You take the root, "dieci" and add the number that follows. "Dieci" is a word born from the contraction of two words: diez + y. So, basically, it translates as "ten and", as in "ten and eight" (dieciocho).

A similar thing happens to numbers from 21 to 29. We take the root number (veinte) and compress it. Doing this, we create a new root: "veinti".

Twenty	Veinte	Veh-in-teh
Twenty one	Veintiuno	Veh-in-tee-uh-noh
Twenty two	Veintidós	Veh-in-tee-dos
Twenty three	Veintitrés	Veh-in-tee-tres
Twenty four	Veinticuatro	Veh-in-tee-ku-ah-troh
Twenty five	Veinticinco	Veh-in-tee-sin-ko

Twenty six	Veintiséis	Veh-in-tee-seh-is
Twenty seven	Veintisiete	Veh-in-tee-si-eh-teh
Twenty eight	Veintiocho	Veh-in-tee-oh-cho
Twenty nine	Veintinueve	Veh-in-tee-noo-eh-be

Again, it is all about putting "veinti" and a number, together. Don't worry. Things get way easier from now on.

Thirty	Treinta	Treh-in-tah
Thirty one	Treinta y uno	Tre-in-tah-e-uh-no
Thirty two	Treinta y dos	Tre-in-tah-e-dos

Starting on 30, numbers translate the same way they do for English. "Thirty + number" (30 + number). This way we get "treinta y cinco" (35), "cuarenta y cuatro" (44), "sesenta y yo" (60) or "ciento cuatro" (104).

Fourty	Cuarenta	Ku-ah-ren-tah
Fifty	Cincuenta	Sin-kuen-tah
Sixty	Sesenta	Seh-sen-tah
Seventy	Setenta	Seh-ten-tah
Eighty	Ochenta	Oh-chen-tah
Ninety	Noventa	No-ven-tah
One-hundred	Cien	Sien
One thousand	Mil	Mill

How is this going for you? Don't worry. This is one of those cases where you repeat and repeat, and in time you get it.

Let's move on to ordinal numbers. As the name suggests, they tell the "order" of things. That way, we can make ranks, prioritize, and set dates. Awesome, uh?

First	Primero	Pree-meh-roh

Second	Segundo	Seh-goon-doh
Third	Tercero	Ter-seh-roh
Fourth	Cuarto	Kuar-toh
Fifth	Quinto	Kin-toh
Sixth	Sexto	Sex-toh
Seventh	Séptimo	Sep-tee-moh
Eighth	Octavo	Ok-tah-boh
Ninth	Noveno	Noh-beh-noh

As is the case with cardinal numbers, each of the first ten ordinal numbers has a distinct form. Yet, you will see how easy this gets from now on.

Tenth	Décimo	The-see-moh
Eleventh	Décimo primero	The-see-moh-pree-meh-roh

Twelfth	Décimo segundo	The-see-moh-seh-goon-doh
Thirteenth	Décimo tercero	The-see-moh-ter-seh-roh
Fourteenth	Décimo cuarto	The-see-moh-kuar-toh
Fifteenth	Décimo quinto	The-see-moh-kin-toh

Starting on the 10th, there is a very easy formula. Just as we did with the cardinal numbers over 30, you split the number into two different parts and translate it. For example, 15th is the result of adding the 10th + the 5th. That way you get "Décimo quinto".

The 19th, therefore, is the combination of 10th and 9th. That way we get "Décimo noveno".

Easy right?

Chapter 7 – What did you want to be when you grow?

"What did you want to be when you grew up?" How many times did someone ask you this question when you were a child? How many times have you changed your answer?

When I was little, I wanted to be a scientist. Later on, I wanted to be a singer. Nowadays I am a writer, but previously I have had different jobs. I have been a teacher, an electrician – honestly, not a very good one- and a chef.

We always need to remember that all professions are important. We need farmers to produce food of the highest quality, doctors to treat injuries and disease, artists to represent the beauty of the world around us, and bilingual writers to write Spanish for Beginners.

Speaking of artists, this is a good word to start with.

Artist	Artista
Picasso was an **artist**.	Picasso fue un **artista**.

R-tees-tah

You should always keep in mind that vowels like "a" are very open and clear in Spanish. "A" is pronounced like the English word "ah!". "Artista"

Chef	Cocinero
I want to become a **chef**.	Yo quiero convertirme en **cocinero**.

Ko-si-neh-ro

Construction worker	Obrero

| My dad is a **construction worker**. | Mi papá es un **obrero**. |

Oh-breh-roh

The Spanish "O" is also a very open vowel.

| Firefighter | Bombero |
| Being a **firefighter** is a risky job. | Ser **bombero** es un trabajo peligroso. |

Bom-beh-roh

| Doctor | Doctor |
| The **doctor** will see you in 5 minutes. | La **doctora** lo atenderá en 5 minutos. |

Doc-toh-rah

Unlike the English word "doctor", in the Spanish, the strong syllable is the second. Doc-tor.

| Policeman | Policía |

| A **policeman** came to our house. | Un **policía** vino a nuestra casa. |

Po-lee-c-ah

Teacher	Profesor
That is my **teacher**.	Esa es mi **profesora**.

Pro-phe-soh-rah

Let's put effort into this single "r". Proh-phe-soh-rah

Actor/Actress	Actor/Actriz
Emma Stone is an **actress**.	Emma Stone es una **actriz**.

Ac-trees

Banker	Banquero
I am waiting for a **banker**.	Estoy esperando por un **banquero**.

Ban-ke-roh

Butcher	Carnicero
I am calling the **butcher** to order.	Estoy llamando al **carnicero** para ordenar.

Kar-nee-se-roh

Dentist	Dentista
I have a great **dentist.**	Tengo un gran **dentista.**

Den-tees-tah

Driver	Conductor
My **driver** is very fast.	Mi **conductor** es muy rápido.

Kon-dook-tor

How's that buzzing in your palate?

Electrician	Electricista
You need to call the **electrician**.	Necesitas llamar al **electricista**.

www.LearnLikeNatives.com

Eh-lek-tree-cis-tah

Farmer	Granjero
My grandpa was a **farmer**.	Mi abuelo era **granjero**.

Gran-he-roh

Hairdresser	Estilista
I have a great **hairdresser**.	Yo tengo un gran **estilista**.

S-t-lis-tah

Journalist	Periodista
I will be a **journalist**.	Yo seré un **periodista**.

Pe-ree-oh-dees-tah

Lawyer	Abogado
My daughter is a **lawyer**.	Mi hija es **abogada**.

Ah-boh-ga-dah

Painter	Pintor
That **painter** did a good job.	Ese **pintor** hizo un buen trabajo.

Peen-tor

There are plenty of professions but don't worry, we won't go through them all. Just few more words.

Politician	Político
I want to be a **politician**.	Yo quiero ser un **político**.

Po-li-ti-coh

Psychologist	Psicólogo
I am a **psychologist**.	Yo soy **psicólogo**.

Si-ko-lo-go

Scientist	Científico

Scientists are addressing climate change.	Los **científicos** están abordando el cambio climático.

Sien-ti-fee-ko

What did you want to be when you grew up? Let's learn a few more words.

Plumber	Plomero
I have to call the **plumber.**	Tengo que llamar al **plomero**.

Ploh-meh-roh

Secretary	Secretario
My **secretary** is on vacation.	Mi **secretario** está de vacaciones.

Se-cre-ta-reeo

Shoemaker	Zapatero

| The **shoemaker** did a good job. | El **zapatero** hizo un buen trabajo. |

Sa-pah-teh-roh

| Singer | Cantante |
| She's a great **singer**. | Ella es una gran **cantante**. |

Kan-tan-teh

| Waiter/Waitress | Mesonero/Mesonera |
| I'll call the **waiter**. | Llamaré al **mesonero**. |

Me-soh-neh-roh

| Writer | Escritor |
| It is hard to be a **writer**. | Es difícil ser una **escritora**. |

S-kri-tor

| Translator | Traductor |

| I work as a **translator**. | Yo trabajo como **traductora**. |

Tra-duk-tor

Let's practice!

Cris: *Hey! What do you have there?*

¡Hola! ¿Qué tienes ahí?

Layla: *It's a firefighter costume.*

Es un disfraz de bombero.

Cris: *Is it November yet?*

¿Ya es Noviembre?

Layla: *No! My son's school is going to have a "career day".*

¡No! La escuela de mi hijo va a tener el "día de la carrera".

Cris: *Oh, I see. I wanted to be a psychologist when I was nine.*

Oh, ya veo. Yo quería ser psicóloga cuando tenía nueve.

Layla: *I wanted to be a teacher. We are always changing, right?*

Yo quería ser una profesora. Siempre estamos cambiando, ¿verdad?

Cris: *Yeah. I wanted to be a teacher when I was fourteen.*

Sí. Yo quería ser profesora cuando tenía catorce.

Layla: *How did you decide to become a lawyer?*

¿Cómo decidiste convertirte en abogada?

Cris: *Well... you know. I was seventeen and wanted to change the world.*

Bueno... tú sabes. Tenía diecisiete y quería cambiar el mundo.

Layla: *My son wants to be a farmer.*

Mi hijo quiere ser granjero.

Cris: *Isn't his dad a politician?*

¿No es su papá un político?

Layla: *Yeah. He started as a journalist and then changed careers.*

Sí. Él comenzó como periodista y luego cambió de carrera.

Cris: *Indeed. We are always changing.*

Efectivamente. Siempre estamos cambiando.

Now, repeat with me: "I wanted to be" -" Yo quería ser un" and complete the sentence.

One of the first questions people ask to someone they have just met is "What is your job?" which translates to "Che lavoro fai?". Thanks to what we have just learned in this unit, you are going to be ready for this conversation!

What next? Let's learn how to ask for directions.

www.LearnLikeNatives.com

Chapter 8 – Where are we going?

Being able to clearly tell where you want to go is very important, especially when traveling in another country. For this reason, the ability to communicate in simple situations such as asking for directions can make your life easier, in case of a SatNav failure or during a relaxing afternoon walk, when you don't have your mobile with you.

Street	Calle
That is the main **street**.	Esa es la **calle** principal.

Ka-ie

Avenue	Avenida
This is Libertador **Avenue**.	Esta es la **Avenida** Libertador.

A-ve-nee-da

Block	Cuadra

| We are going to the **block** party. | Nosotros vamos a la fiesta de la **cuadra**. |

Kua-drah

| Square | Plaza |
| The **square** should be a few blocks ahead. | La **plaza** debería estar algunas cuadras más adelante. |

Plah-sah

Are you pronouncing those vowels properly? Remember the open vowels!

| Building | Edificio |
| This **building** has 110 floors. | Este **edificio** tiene 110 pisos. |

E-dee-fee-sio

| Monument | Monumento |

This **monument** is 300 years old.	Este **monumento** tiene 300 años.

Mo-nu-men-to

Hospital	Hospital
The **hospital** is 5 minutes away.	El **hospital** está a 5 minutos.

Hos-pi-tal

Unlike the English "hospital", in Spanish, the strong syllable is "tal". The last syllable. In addition, make sure to make a clear "t". Hos-pi-tal.

Corner	Esquina
The store is passing that **corner**.	La tienda está pasando esa **esquina**.

Es-ki-nah

Nearest	Más cercano

| That is the **nearest** mall. | Ese es el centro comercial **más cercano**. |

Mas-ser-kah-no

| Turn left | Girar a la izquierda |
| You should **turn left** in two blocks. | Deberías **girar a la izquierda** en dos cuadras. |

Hi-rar-ah-lah-is-ki-er-dah

| Turn right | Girar a la derecha |
| Let's **turn right** after this corner. | Vamos a **girar a la derecha** luego de esta esquina. |

Hi-rar-ah-lah-deh-reh-chah

| Go straight on | Seguir recto |
| You only have to **go straight** on and you will get there. | Solo debes **seguir recto** y llegarás. |

Se-geer-rrek-toh

"Recto" has a strong double "r" sound in its first syllable, unlike "derecho", which is supposed to have only a soft "r" sound in its second one.

Go past	Pasar
You have to **go past** the main street.	Tienes que **pasar** la calle principal.

Pah-sar

Crossroads	Encrucijada
Take the left on the **crossroads.**	Toma la izquierda en la **encrucijada**.

N-kru-c-ha-dah

Those phrases will take you wherever you desire! Are you ready to put into practice what we have just learned about directions?

John:	¡Hey, sir! Good afternoon.
	¡Hola, señor! Buenas tardes.
Vendor (Vendedor):	What can I do for you?
	¿Qué puedo hacer por ti?
John:	Can you tell me how I can get to the train station?
	¿Puedes decirme cómo llego a la estación de tren?
Vendor	Sure. You have to go in that direction for three blocks.
	Claro. Tienes que ir en esa dirección por tres cuadras.
John:	I have to go past the library?
	¿Tengo que pasar la biblioteca?
Vendor	Yes. Then, you turn left and go for another five or six blocks.

	Sí. Luego doblas a la izquierda y sigues por cinco o seis cuadras.
John:	*Oh, I think I came from there. But I got confused at the crossroads.*
	Oh, creo que vengo de ahí. Pero me confundí en la encrucijada.
Vendor	*Happens all the time(Very usual). You have to go left at the crossroads.*
	Muy usual. Tienes que tomar la izquierda en la encrucijada.
John:	*Ok.*
	Está bien.
Vendor	*You will see a square. The station is in front.*
	Verás una plaza. La estación está al frente.
John:	*Thank you very much.*
	Muchísimas gracias.

Vendor: *No worries. Have a nice trip.*

No te preocupes. Que tengas un feliz viaje.

Are you ready to go and explore a new place? Better hurry! "Survival 101" is coming.

www.LearnLikeNatives.com

Chapter 9 – Survival 101

Each chapter contains helpful information, but this is particularly important. We have already said that: sometimes things go wrong. Your child may feel unwell, you could twist an ankle while hiking, lose your passport.... things do happen. So it's better to be prepared, right?

This sentence is pretty important:

Do you speak English?	¿Hablas español?

Ah-blas-es-pah-niol

This next one will make your life much easier.

Where is the bathroom?	¿Dónde está el baño?

Don-the-s-tah-el-ba-nio

How can I get to this place?	¿Cómo puedo llegar a este lugar?

Ko-moh-pooeh-doh-ie-gar-ah-es-the-loo-gar

| Where is the nearest hospital? | ¿Dónde está el hospital más cercano? |

Don-the-s-tah-el-hos-pee-tal-mas-ser-ka-no

Extremely important: "¿Dónde está el hospital más cercano?".

| When is the next flight? | ¿Cuándo es el próximo vuelo? |

Kuan-doh-es-el-proc-si-moh-vooe-lo

| Who can I talk to about this problem? | ¿Con quién puedo hablar sobre este problema? |

Kon-kien-pooe-doh-ah-blar-soh-bre-es-teh-pro-bleh-mah

| Where can I find a policeman? | ¿Dónde puedo encontrar a un policía? |

Don-the-pooe-do-en-kon-trar-ah-oon-poh-lee-c-a

Though I hope you will never need this:

| Where is the embassy? | ¿Dónde está la embajada? |

Don-the-s-tah-lah-m-bah-ha-da

What do I need to visit...?	¿Qué necesito para visitar...?

Ke-neh-seh-si-toh-pah-rah-bee-ah-har

Where can I find...?	¿Dónde puedo encontrar...?

Don-the-pooe-doh-en-kon-trar

Oh, I really hope you won't need some of them. But better safe than sorry! Let's see a short dialogue now.

Harry: *Hello, sir. How can I get to Kapital Burger, in Dos de Mayo Avenue?*

Hola, señor. ¿Cómo puedo llegar a Kapital Burger, en Avenida Dos de Mayo?

Driver: *I can take you, but is far. Is someone waiting for you? It's rush hour.*

Puedo llevarte, pero es lejos. ¿Alguien te está esperando? Es hora pico.

Harry: *No. I think I left my passport there.*

No. Creo que dejé mi pasaporte ahí.

Driver: *It will take us at least 40 minutes to get there.*

Nos tomará al menos 40 minutos llegar hasta allá.

Harry: *Ok. Maybe I can talk to someone there.*

Está bien. Tal vez puedo hablar con alguien ahí.

Vendor: *Good afternoon. Kapital Burger.*

Buenas tardes. Kapital Burger.

Harry: *Hello! My name is Harry Klein. I was there last night, and I think I left my passport.*

¡Hola! Mi nombre es Harry Klein. Estuve ahí anoche, y creo que dejé mi pasaporte.

Vendor: *One second, please. Do you remember where were you sitting?*

Un Segundo, por favor. ¿Usted recuerda dónde estaba sentado?

Harry: *Yes. I was at the bar, by the corner.*

Sí. Estaba en el bar, hacia la esquina.

Vendor: *Ok. Give me a second.*

Está bien. Dame un segundo.

Harry: *Ok.*

Está bien.

Vendor: *Yeah. I just consulted my coworkers and they did not find anything. I am sorry.*

Sí. Acabo de consultar a mis compañeros de trabajo y no consiguieron nada. Lo siento.

Harry: *Thank you.*

Gracias.

Driver: *They didn't find it?*

¿No lo encontraron?

Harry: *No. Where is the nearest police station?*

No. ¿Dónde está la estación de policía más cercana?

Driver: *Don't you want to go to your embassy? Could be better.*

¿No quieres ir a tu embajada? Podría ser mejor.

Harry: *Oh, yes. Where's the UK embassy?*

Oh, sí. ¿Dónde está la embajada del Reino Unido?

Driver: *Actually, it is near here. We will be there in a few minutes.*

De hecho, es cerca de aquí. Estaremos ahí en unos minutos.

What a nightmare to lose your passport abroad! I sincerely hope you will never have to use some of these phrases.

Now, let's move on to something less stressful. Shall we switch to colors?

Chapter 10 – What is the color of the sky?

I will tell you a secret: I love a wonderful view, and everywhere I go, I like to just lose myself gazing at the sky. I particularly love the sunset. I also like the sunrise, but I'm really not a morning person.

How many colors are there in the sky?

Yellow	Amarillo

| My dress is **yellow**. | Mi vestido es **amarillo**. |

Ah-mah-ree-io

Blue	Azul
The sky looks very **blue**.	El cielo luce muy **azul**.

Ah-sul

Red	Rojo
I bought a **red** car.	Yo compré un auto **rojo**.

Rro-ho

Purple	Púrpura
Those flowers are **purple**.	Esas flores son **púrpura**.

Poor-poo-rah

Pink	Rosa
My daughter wants a **pink** gown.	Mi hija quiere un atuendo **rosa**.

Roh-sah

Green	Verde
The fields look very **green** this year.	Los campos lucen bastante **verdes** este año.

Ber-des

Practice that "r" sound.

Orange	Naranja
I want my **orange** t-shirt.	Yo quiero mi camiseta **naranja**.

Nah-ran-ha

Brown	Marrón
Your dog is **brown**.	Tu perro es **marrón**.

Ma-run

Grey	Gris

Grey is a mixed color.	El **gris** es un color combinado.

Grease

Black	Negro
Black is my favorite color.	El **negro** es mi color favorito.

Neh-groh

White	Blanco
I painted the walls **white**.	Pinté las paredes de **blanco**.

Blan-ko

Fun fact: black and white are not colors. They represent, respectively, the absence of light and the lack of shadow.

No prizes for guessing what is coming now… Let's practice!

Lisa: *Hey, honey! I need your help with something.*

Hola, cariño. Necesito tu ayuda con algo.

Alex: *Yes, love. What is it?*

Sí, amor. ¿De qué se trata?

Lisa: *We need to pick the colors for the house before we move.*

Tenemos que escoger los colores para la casa antes de mudarnos.

Alex: *Oh, true. What do you have in mind?*

Oh, cierto. ¿Qué tienes en mente?

Lisa: *I was thinking of a light blue for our room, with touches of yellow.*

Estaba pensando en un azul claro para nuestro cuarto, con toques de amarillo.

Alex: *Ok. What have you thought of the living room?*

Está bien. ¿Qué has pensado para la sala?

Lisa: *I am thinking of a combination of red and white walls.*

Estoy pensando en una combinación de paredes rojas y blancas.

Alex: Do you think that my black chair will match?

¿Tú crees que mi silla negra combinará?

Lisa: Absolutely(positive). And for the studio, I was looking for something more neutral.

Positivo. Y para el estudio, estaba buscando algo más neutral.

Alex: By neutral you mean...?

¿Por neutral quieres decir...?

Lisa: Earth colors. Like a light brown.

Colores tierra. Como un marron claro.

Alex: And the nursery?

¿Y para el cuarto del bebé?

Lisa: Grey, with a purple wall.

Gris, con una pared púrpura.

Alex: *It sounds amazing. Thanks for planning all this.*

Suena asombroso. Gracias por planear todo esto.

Lisa: *Sure! I love it!*

¡Claro! ¡Me encanta!

What about you? Are you already planning to repaint your whole house? And for your dining room, would you like to go and buy some lanterns at an artisanal market in Mexico? Imagine all the things you could do! First of all, however, we need to get there. Let's go!

Chapter 11 – So much to do, so much to see

Where do you dream of going? Personally, I love the mountains. I grew up in a village in the valley, with stunning views of the mountains. I think maybe that's why I love mountains so much!

Now, imagine where you would like to go

Travel	Viaje
She lost the scarf during her last **trip**.	Ella perdió la bufanda durante su último **viaje**.

Bee-ah-he

Ticket	Boleto
I bought a two-way **ticket**.	Yo compré un **boleto** de ida y vuelta.

Boh-leh-toh

Airplane	Avión
This **airplane** is big.	Este **avión** es grande.

Ah-bee-on

Reservation	Reservación
He made a **reservation** for tonight.	Él hizo una **reservación** para esta noche.

Rre-ser-bah-sion

Re-ser-va-ción. Notice that accent in the last syllable.

Hotel	Hotel
I like this **hotel**.	A mí me gusta este **hotel**.

Ho-tel

Room	Habitación
They need a double **room**.	Ellos necesitan una **habitación** doble.

Ha-bee-ta-sion

Key	Llave
I lost my **key**.	Yo perdí mi **llave**.

Ya-beh

Passport	Pasaporte
Can I see your **passport**?	Puedo ver su **pasaporte**?

Pah-sah-por-te

Taxi	Taxi
Let's take a **taxi**.	Vamos a tomar un **taxi**.

Tac-si

"Taxi" is the same both in Italian and in English.

Car rental	Alquiler de autos
Where is the **car rental**?	¿Dónde está el **alquiler de autos**?

Al-ki-ler-the-au-tos

Bus	Autobús
We will take the **bus**.	Nosotros tomaremos el **autobús**.

Auto-bus

Subway	Subterráneo
The **subway** was out of service.	El **subterráneo** estaba fuera de servicio.

Sub-teh-rra-neo

Train	Tren
I'll take the **train**.	Yo tomaré el **tren**.

Tren

Let the "t" help you boosting the "r".

Station	Estación
That is the nearest **station**.	Esa es la **estación** más cercana.

Es-tah-sion

Theater	Teatro
This **theater** was remodeled 5 years ago.	Este **teatro** fue remodelado hace 5 años.

Teh-ah-tro

Beach	Playa
She wants to go to the **beach**.	Ella quiere ir a la **playa**.

Pla-ya

Mountain	Montaña
They want to climb that **mountain.**	Ellos quieren escalar esa **montaña**.

Mon-ta-niah

How is the "ñ" working for you' Have you been trying? Come on! Mon-ta-niah.

Island	Isla

www.LearnLikeNatives.com

Let's go to that **island**.	Vamos a esa **isla**.

Ees-lah

City	Ciudad
Mexico has big **cities**.	México tiene grandes **ciudades**.

Siu-dah-des

Are you ready? You know the drill. It's time to practice.

Shaun: *I want to buy the tickets for our trip. Can we decide on something?*

Quiero comprar los boletos para nuestro viaje. ¿Podemos decidir algo?

Vanessa: *Sure! Where do we want to go?*

¡Claro! ¿A dónde queremos ir?

Shaun: *Not another city. I want to rest.*

No a otra ciudad. Quiero descansar.

Vanessa: I agree. Do you remember that beautiful mountain that Lisa showed us? Navarino Island.

Estoy de acuerdo. ¿Tú recuerdas esa hermosa montaña que Lisa nos mostró? Isla Navarino.

Shaun: Oh, sure. That cozy mountain house, right?

Oh, por supuesto. Esa acogedora casa de montaña, ¿verdad?

Vanessa: Yes. That one.

Sí. Esa.

Shaun: That sounds great. Do you think it is available?

Eso suena genial. ¿Crees que esté disponible?

Vanessa: On it!

¡Estoy en eso!

Shaun: Remember to check for a view.

Recuerda buscar una vista.

Vanessa: *I got the perfect room! It is beautiful.*

Conseguí la habitación perfecta. Es hermosa.

Shaun: *Great. I need our passports to buy the tickets. I'll go get them.*

Genial. Necesito nuestros pasaportes para comprar los boletos. Iré a buscarlos.

Vanessa: *Sure. I am excited!*

Claro. ¡Estoy emocionada!

Repeat with me: "quiero viajar a" –I want to travel to-, then go out and make it happen! Traveling is an amazing way to meet new people and discover beautiful places. In my opinion, traveling is like growing up, except it never has to end.

A spontaneous trip, a last-second vacation… these are usually the best trips, the kind of stories you will remember forever.

And do you know what else I like when traveling? The food!

www.LearnLikeNatives.com

A Quick Message

A quick message before we start the final chapter of this book.

"No one can whistle a symphony. It takes a whole orchestra to play it." –

H.E. Luccock

Do you want to be part of the orchestra of the Learning Spanish community?

Here is how:

If you're enjoying this book, I would like to kindly ask you to leave a brief review on Amazon.

Reviews aren't easy to come by, but they have a profound impact in supporting my work. This way, I can keep creating new content to help the whole community at my very best.

I would be incredibly thankful if you could just take a minute to leave a quick review on Amazon, even if it's just a sentence or two!

www.LearnLikeNatives.com

It's that simple!

Thank you so much for taking the time to leave a short review on Amazon.

The community and I are very appreciative, as your review makes a difference.

Now, let's get back to learning Spanish!

Chapter 12 – I have a little craving

Food is a language itself. Food talks about soils, about culture, and about lifestyle. Whenever going to new places, having local food is fundamental for a trip that is complete.

However, we will let the locals introduce you to their exotic dishes. I will teach you some basics, though.

Potato	Papa

| I want **potato** fries. | Yo quiero **papas** fritas. |

Pah-pahs

| Tomato | Tomate |
| You only need a few **tomatoes**. | Tú solo necesitas algunos **tomates**. |

Toh-mah-tes

| Corn | Maíz |
| Mexicans eat a lot of **corn**. | Los mexicanos comen bastante **maíz**. |

Ma-ees

"Maíz" is fundamental. Mexicans discovered that corn is a very versatile ingredient.

| Egg | Huevo |
| She wants **eggs** and ham. | Ella quiere **huevos** y jamón. |

Ooe-boss

Cheese	Queso
I don't eat **cheese**.	Yo no como **queso**.

Ke-soh

Butter	Mantequilla
French people love **butter.**	Los franceses aman la **mantequilla**.

Man-te-ki-ya

"Man-te-qui-lla". Great for your taste buds.

Sandwich	Emparedado
We want five regular **sandwiches**.	Nosotros queremos cinco **emparedados** regulares.

Em-pa-reh-dah-dos

Burger	Hamburguesa

| They want three **burgers**. | Ellos quieren tres **hamburguesas**. |

Am-boor-ghe-sas

See?

| Salad | Ensalada |
| I want a Caesar **salad.** | Yo quiero una **ensalada** César. |

N-sa-lah-dah

| Shrimp | Camarón |
| It has **shrimps** inside. | Eso tiene **camarones** adentro. |

Ka-ma-roh-nes

Say again with me: ka-ma-roh-nes.

| Sausage | Salchicha |

We love **sausages** for breakfast.	Nosotros amamos las **salchichas** en el desayuno.

Sal-chee-chas

Bread	Pan
I bought the **bread** this morning.	Yo compré el **pan** esta mañana.

Pan

Chicken	Pollo
That **chicken** is raw.	Ese **pollo** está crudo.

Poh-io

Pancakes	Panqueques
These **pancakes** are fluffy.	Estos **panqueques** están esponjosos.

Pan-ke-kes

Rice	Arroz

| The **rice** is ready. | El **arroz** está listo. |

Ah-rros

If you want to eat rice, you better master that double "r". A-rroz.

| Bacon | Tocino |
| The flavor of **bacon** is delicious. | El sabor del **tocino** es delicioso. |

Toh-c-noh

| Milk | Leche |
| I think this **milk** has gone bad. | Yo creo que esta **leche** se ha estropeado. |

Leh-cheh

The "ch" sound in Spanish, is quite similiar to the English one. Our "ch" is the sound you would use to say "church", for example.

Cake	Pastel
You can eat more **cake**.	Tú puedes comer más **pastel**.

Pas-tel

Soup	Sopa
This **soup** is hot.	Esta **sopa** está caliente.

Soh-pah

Onion	Cebolla
I was chopping **onions**.	Yo estaba cortando **cebollas**.

Se-boh-yas

The Spanish sound for a double "l" is similar to the "y" in English, like in the word "yes".

Garlic	Ajo

| You need to add **garlic** and stir. | Necesitas agregar **ajo** y remover. |

Ah-ho

| Lemon | Limón |
| These **lemons** look very nice. | Estos **limones** se ven muy bien. |

Lee-moh-ness

| Orange | Naranja |
| I want **orange** juice, please. | Yo quiero jugo de **naranja**, por favor. |

Nah-ran-ha

| Peanut | Maní |
| I am allergic to **peanuts**. | Soy alérgico al **maní**. |

Mah-nee

"Maní" is an important one. It is, after all, one of the most common allergies around the world.

We are so close to finishing this first level!

Let's practice! Just one more!

Veronica: *I am hungry.*

Estoy hambrienta.

Karol: *Let's see. There are still eggs, cheese and bread from the breakfast.*

Veamos. Todavía hay huevos, queso y pan del desayuno.

Veronica: *Uhm... Do we have potatoes and onions? It could use the eggs.*

Uhm... ¿Tenemos papas y cebollas? Podría usar los huevos.

Karol: *No. I couldn't go grocery shopping yesterday.*

No. No pude ir de compras ayer.

Veronica: *It's fine. Maybe I could go to that sandwich place, by the corner.*

Está bien. Tal vez podría ir a ese lugar de emparedados, en la esquina.

Karol: *I don't think it is open yet.*

Yo no creo que esté abierto todavía.

Veronica: *Oh... I could go for burgers, then. Do you want anything?*

Oh... Podría ir por hamburguesas, entonces. ¿Quieres algo?

Karol: *That sounds nice! Can you get me a salad?*

¡Eso suena bien! ¿Podrías traerme una ensalada?

Veronica: *Sure! What kind of salad would you like?*

¡Seguro! ¿Qué tipo de ensalada te gustaría?

Karol: *Maybe a chicken Caesar salad.*

Tal vez una ensalada César con pollo.

Veronica: *Sounds good. I will come back soon.*

Suena bien. Volveré pronto.

How did this feel? I bet it was not that hard. I hope I am right because food is very important. Right?

Conclusion

Congratulations, you've made it! See, it wasn't too hard, was it?

As you realized by now, this wasn't your typical language book. If you tried and failed to learn Spanish in the past, you now discovered a new approach, one that you can build on to take your Spanish adventure to the next level. In going away from formal vocabulary and grammar lessons, together we shifted your focus from 'learning' Spanish to 'speaking' Spanish. Two very different things!

More than just the "rules" of Spanish grammar, today you have a sense of "the soul and music" of the Spanish language. You built a true solid foundation in Spanish and, even if you don't realize it yet, you are now capable of navigating social situations, create connections, keep contacts, as well as make friends. As I mentioned at the start, what's the point in knowing grammatical rules if you can't order your own food!

I won't bore you with the reasons why being able to speak another language is a huge benefit for you. Or why Spanish in particular will open a world of opportunities. I'm sure you're already convinced! But learning a new language is indeed a complex and rich experience, making this book a journey – your journey – into a new culture.

A beautiful culture you're now a part of.

No one is ever 'ready', so get out there! Travel, read fiction and newspapers in Spanish, watch films, eat Latin American and Spanish foods, make Spanish friends, and immerse yourself in Spanish-speaking cultures. Sure, you'll make a few mistakes at first. But who cares! You can always go back through our lessons and keep building your confidence. I'm sure you'll get there in no time.

This is just the first volume of this series, all packed full of vocabulary and dialogs, covering essential, everyday Spanish that will ensure you master the basics.

You can find the rest of the books in the series, as well as a whole host of other resources, at LearnLikeNatives.com. Simply add the book to your library to take the next step in your language learning journey. If you are ever in need of new

www.LearnLikeNatives.com

ideas or direction, refer to our 'Speak Like a Native' eBook, available to you for free at **LearnLikeNatives.com**, which clearly outlines practical steps you can take to continue learning any language you choose.

A language should be lived, not just learned. So learn it, live it and, most importantly, enjoy it!

www.LearnLikeNatives.com

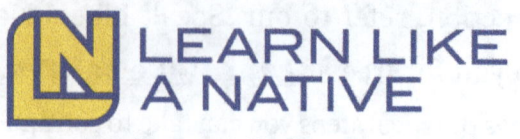

www.LearnLikeNatives.com

Learn Like a Native is a revolutionary **language education brand** that is taking the linguistic world by storm. Forget boring grammar books that never get you anywhere, Learn Like a Native teaches you languages in a fast and fun way that actually works!

As an international, multichannel, language learning platform, we provide **books, audio guides and eBooks** so that you can acquire the knowledge you need, swiftly and easily.

Our **subject-based learning**, structured around real-world scenarios, builds your conversational muscle and ensures you learn the content most relevant to your requirements.
Discover our tools at **LearnLikeNatives.com**

When it comes to learning languages, we've got you covered!

www.ingramcontent.com/pod-product-compliance
Lightning Source LLC
Chambersburg PA
CBHW072202100526
44589CB00015B/2326